Birds & Bees

& Butterflies Too

A Sequel to Frogs & Flowers

by
Camille Remme

ME Publications
1606 Santa Monica Blvd.
Santa Monica, CA 90404
(800) 527-2665

Acknowledgments

All quilts were designed, pieced, and quilted by the author.
Photography by Kathleen Bellesiles, Toronto, Ontario.
Graphic Design and Layout by SPPS Inc., Las Vegas, NV 89130.

ISBN: 0-929950-10-0.

Printed in Hong Kong.

Table of Contents

Table of Contents (continued)

About This Book

❖ The instructions in this book are aimed at the intermediate quilter; that is, someone who uses a rotary cutter and has a sense that any diagram on graph paper can be interpreted by cutting fabric into strips. The innovative sewing techniques needed for design details are covered in this book.

❖ All diagrams were drawn on graph paper with 1 square = 1". Therefore, all blocks will be made by cutting 1½" strips or 2½" strips, assuming ¼" seam allowances.

❖ Efficiency is achieved through the production of many identical blocks (i.e., cutting strips and pieces for many at one time.)

❖ Many designs can also be made in reverse. Since the cutting of the pieces remains the same, cutting may be done before determining whether some will be made in reverse.

❖ For example, if 12 blocks are needed for a pattern and 6 probably will be made in reverse, the cutting for all 12 will be identical. Only at the time of sewing will some steps be reversed. Diagrams should always be followed for either variation of the block.

❖ Although many patterns are included for using the bird, bee, butterfly, and leaf blocks, these blocks may be used in the patterns from my earlier book, *Frogs & Flowers*.

❖ Fabric requirements are not given for any projects. This is because an intermediate quilter usually has a fabric stash to draw from. Also, many projects use small amounts of a variety of fabrics. 1- or 2-yard pieces of background fabrics may be needed for some patterns.

❖ Representing birds exactly as they are in nature is not necessary in these quilt patterns, nor sometimes worth the effort. If you research a bird in a book, you probably will quickly forget some or all of the details. These designs are not meant to be exact representations, but *impressions*.

❖ Although I am not a bird watcher, beekeeper, or butterfly enthusiast, creating these designs has enhanced my awareness and appreciation of these wonderful parts of nature.

❖ Using these designs can be more than just making a quilt block: Experience creating a bird, a bee, or a butterfly for someone you love.

Construction Notes

❖ Sewing breakdowns are given in the simplest form of a block design. If you wish to increase the design elements (e.g., make different wings), redraw the block in order to have an exact visual diagram to follow.

❖ All final blocks are constructed by sewing square and rectangle pieces together.

❖ Various design techniques are used to alter the front of the squares and rectangles before they are sewn together.

❖ Before sewing the squares and rectangles together into a block, you should have a game plan. Look at the block breakdown until the best sewing order becomes evident.

❖ Block breakdowns are given for only one direction. To make the block in reverse (mirror image), you will cut the pieces the same, but you will sew them together differently. *Work visually* with a diagram in front of you.

❖ Many blocks may be broken down further to add color, texture, and extra design details.

❖ All triangles in the block diagrams are made by sewing squares diagonally onto square or rectangle pieces. See *Specific Design Details*, page 47, for instructions.

❖ To start a set of blocks, work logically and efficiently:
   • Choose the fabrics for the design.
   • Have a large board and a diagram at hand.
   • Cut required strip(s) from the fabrics. Cut required pieces from the strips and place them on the board.
   • Carry the diagram and the board containing the cut pieces to the sewing machine.
   • Sew the blocks together in a logical sequence, finger pressing, trimming, and laying them back into place regularly.
   • Make many identical blocks at the same time for increased efficiency.

❖ When following a quilt pattern, make all the required blocks, put the blocks plus the background strips into place on a design wall, and stand back to view the entire pattern. Decide now if you want to change or enlarge the quilt top before you start the final sewing.

Poster-Size Quilts

❖ When I lecture and teach, I stress the value of making poster-size quilts (i.e., quilts from 15" x 20" to about 35" x 45"). By designing and making this size project, I have accelerated my growth in the areas of design skills, color awareness, and sewing techniques.

❖ Working poster-size is liberating because you can be more daring with ideas, since projects do not require a lot of time. Think of smaller projects as learning tools and be more playful in color and design.

❖ Most of my poster-size quilts are used extensively. They are hung in smaller areas such as bathrooms and halls, and they are also easier to share with others than are standard-size quilts.

❖ If something is happening with color or design, make two or three poster-size quilts to further explore the concept. Two or three exploratory pieces make a wonderful grouping in place of a large quilt.

❖ I design most of my projects small. Designing this size project gets me going. Then if something starts to happen in color or design while I am making the project, I will allow the quilt top to evolve to its appropriate size.

❖ Finally, by starting to make only poster-size quilts, my intuition tricks me into creating unplanned large quilts. If you think in terms of poster-size quilts, you may help liberate your color and design skills.

Developing Intuition

❖ One way to enhance creativity is to develop and trust your intuition. This gets into the realm of getting in touch with your feelings and trusting them. It can mean trying out many ideas until one *feels* right. This also allows for new possibilities to emerge when you least expect them. Intuition is closely tied to right brain skills, from which creativity stems. The opposite, of course, are logical left brain skills.

❖ Intuition serves us when we develop a playful attitude toward color and design selections for our quilts. I have many projects for which I have done thumbnail sketches, pulled fabric, arranged and rearranged fabrics, and looked at for days or weeks, and then not completed. If the project was meant to be completed, it would have happened. Either something else better came along, or the original idea evolved into something better. The exercise is worthwhile, even if the quilt does not get made, because it helps develop a quilter's intuition and creativity.

❖ Ideas flow when you are busy, not when you are idle. By having lots of projects and ideas lined up, you complete only the best ones, and keep your creative juices engaged.

Working Visually

❖ As your intuition and creativity grow, you will become very comfortable working visually. Working visually means always having a diagram or block at hand for reference. All construction decisions are made by referring to the visual example you have set up, not by thinking, "What do I do next?"

❖ By always working to duplicate the visual example, I work faster, more efficiently, and with few mistakes. This exercise of always making myself work from a visual has enhanced how I look at a things (e.g., a leaf, a tree, a person). Developing this skill has added to my life in many unexpected ways far beyond my quilting skills. Growth in any area of your life often can spill over into other, unexpected areas. Please develop enhanced visual skills and open up new possibilities for yourself.

The Blocks

All dimensions in this section
represent *finished* sizes.

Miscellaneous Birds

5" x 5"

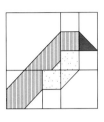 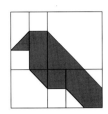 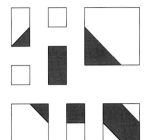

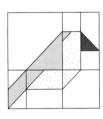 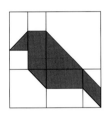 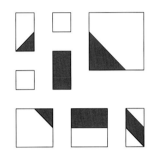

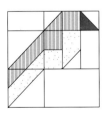 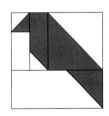 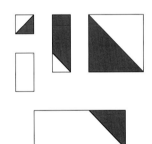

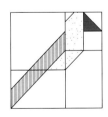 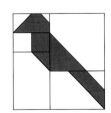 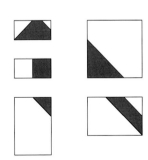

❖ Only Silhouette Piecing Shown
❖ Redraw to Add Details or Make in Reverse

Miscellaneous Birds (continued)

5" x 5"

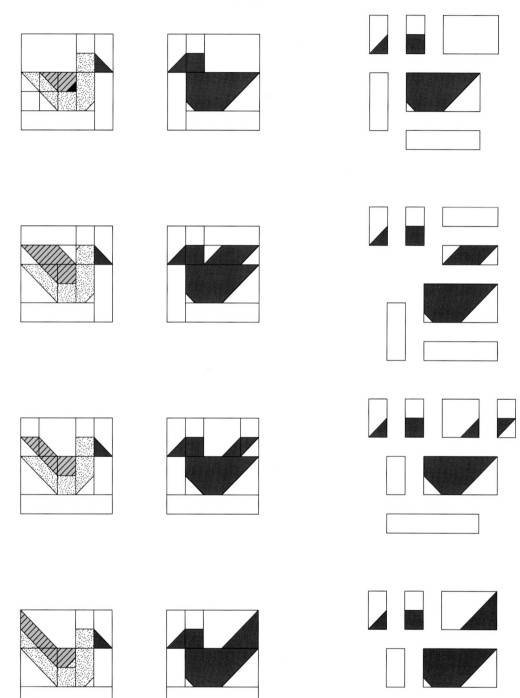

❖ Only Silhouette Piecing Shown
❖ Redraw to Add Details or Make in Reverse

Miscellaneous Birds (continued)

5" x 5"

 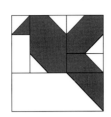 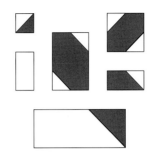

 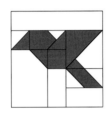 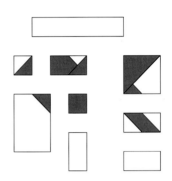

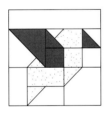 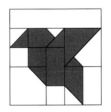 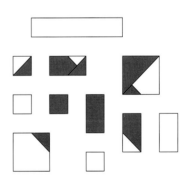

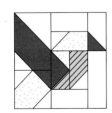 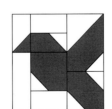 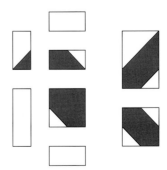

❖ Only Silhouette Piecing Shown
❖ Redraw to Add Details or Make in Reverse

Miscellaneous Birds (continued)
5" x 5"

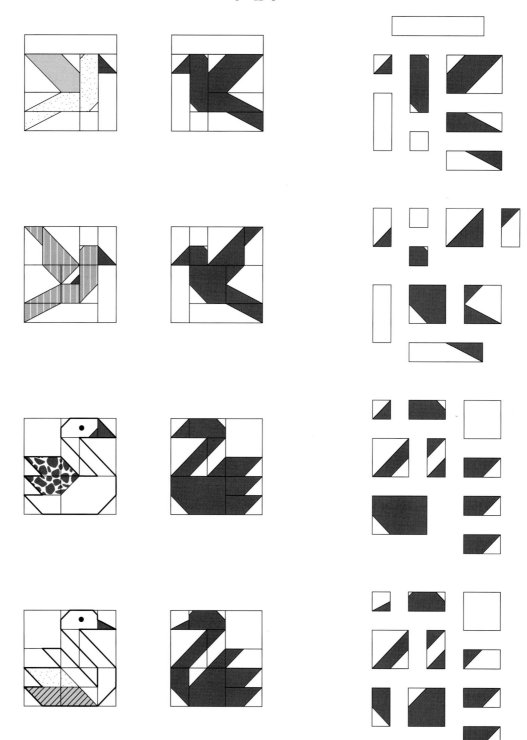

❖ Only Silhouette Piecing Shown
❖ Redraw to Add Details or Make in Reverse

Miscellaneous Birds (continued)

5" x 5"

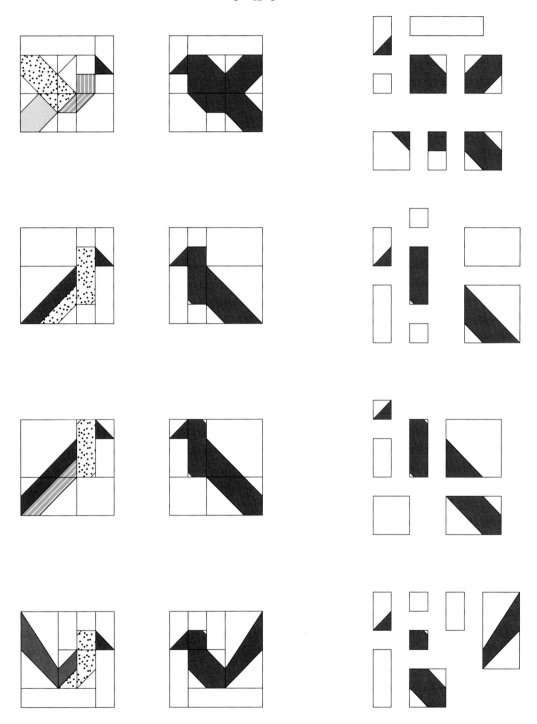

❖ Only Silhouette Piecing Shown
❖ Redraw to Add Details or Make in Reverse

Swans

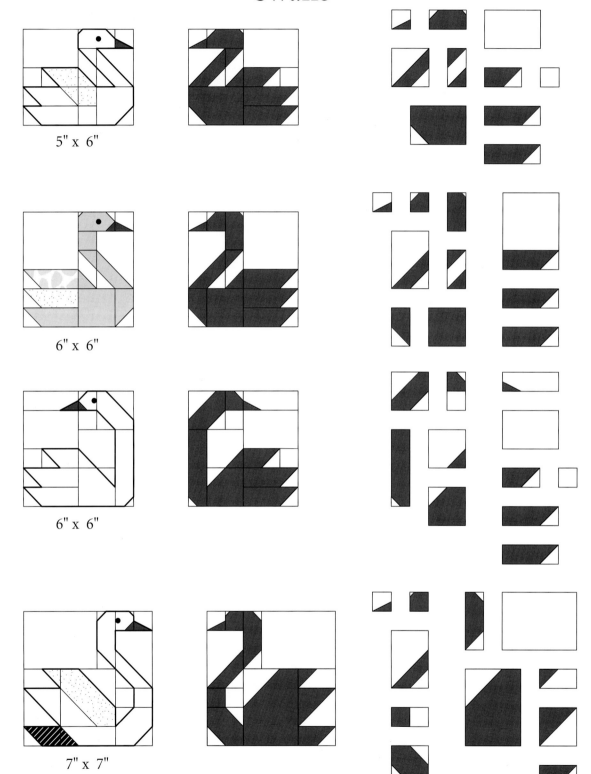

5" x 6"

6" x 6"

6" x 6"

7" x 7"

❖ Only Silhouette Piecing Shown
❖ Redraw to Add Details or Make in Reverse

Swans (continued)

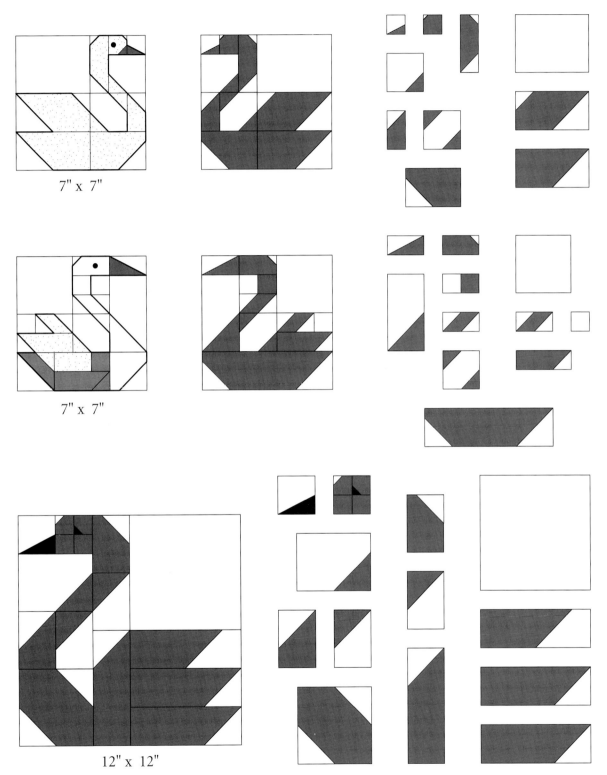

7" x 7"

7" x 7"

12" x 12"

❖ Only Silhouette Piecing Shown
❖ Redraw to Add Details or Make in Reverse

Blue Jays
6" x 10"

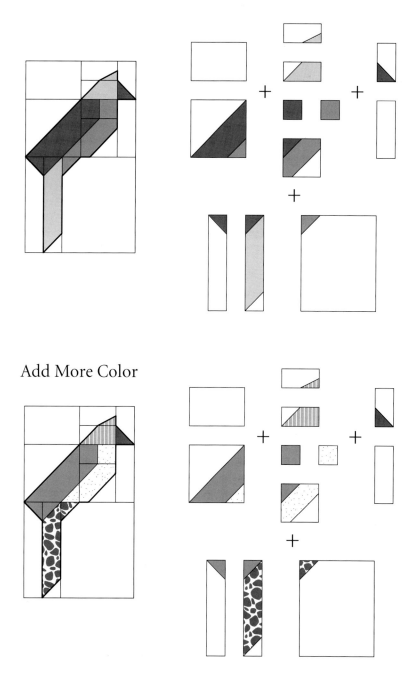

Add More Color

18

Cardinals
6" x 10"

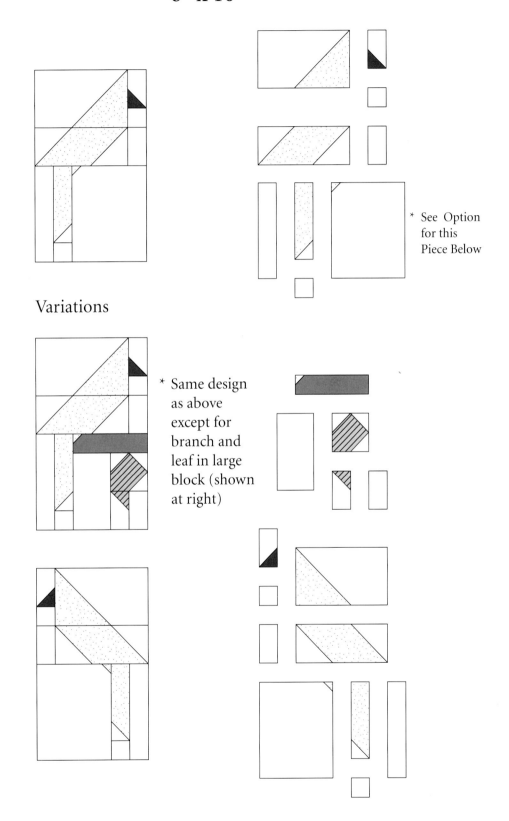

* See Option
  for this
  Piece Below

Variations

* Same design
  as above
  except for
  branch and
  leaf in large
  block (shown
  at right)

Owls

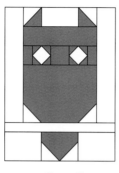

6" x 8"

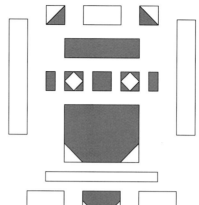

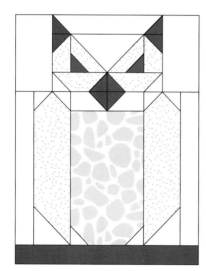

10" x 13"

Flamingos

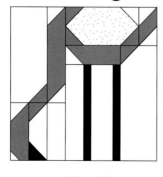

8" x 8"

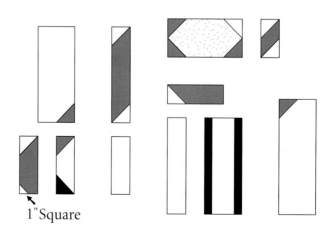

1"Square

Parrots

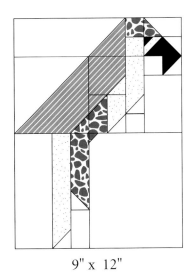

9" x 12"

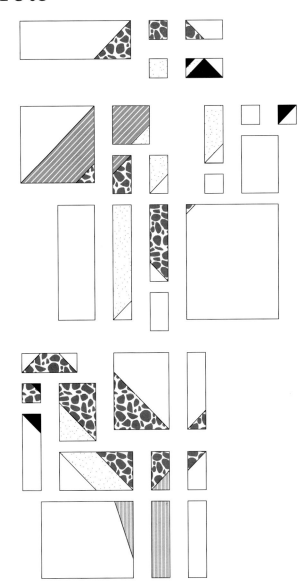

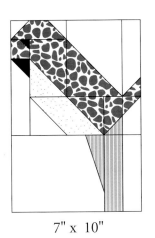

7" x 10"

Toucans

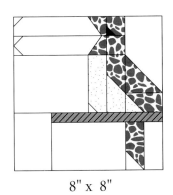

8" x 8"

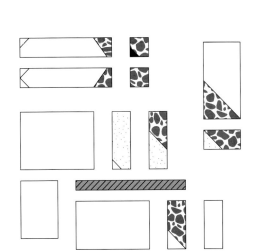

21

Sea Gulls

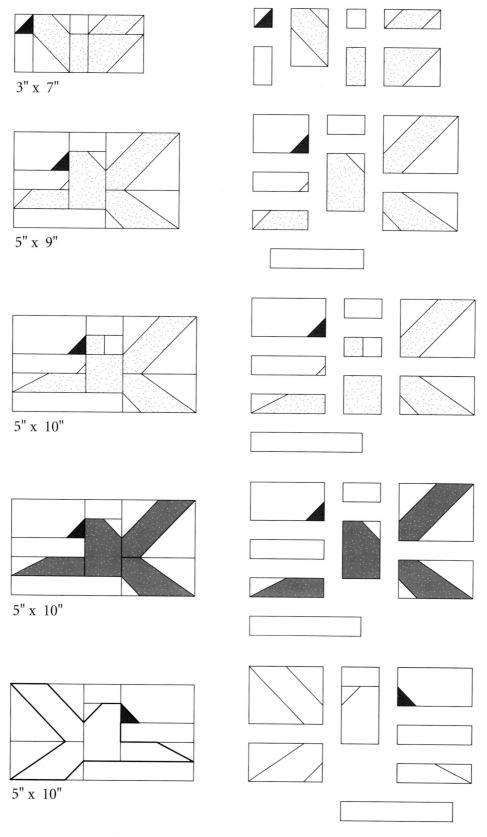

3" x 7"

5" x 9"

5" x 10"

5" x 10"

5" x 10"

22

Ducks

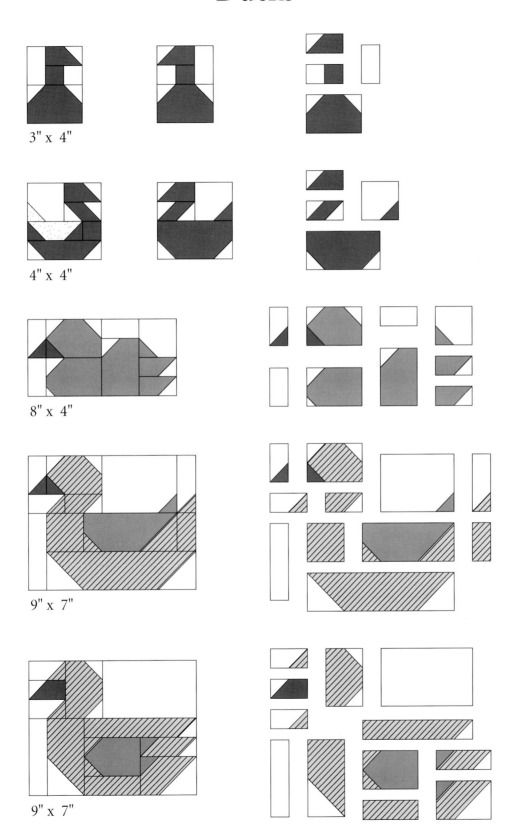

3" x 4"

4" x 4"

8" x 4"

9" x 7"

9" x 7"

Ducks (continued)

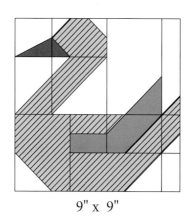

9" x 9"

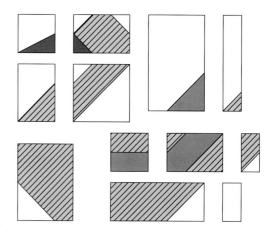

Doves

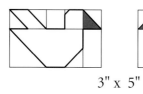

3" x 5"

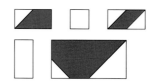

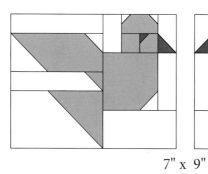

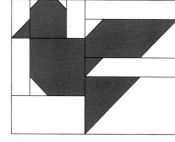

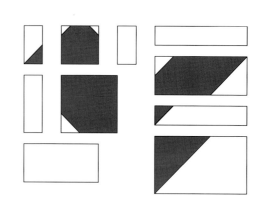

7" x 9"

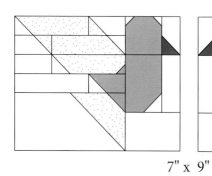

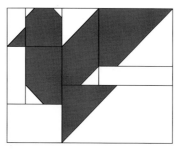

7" x 9"

Bees

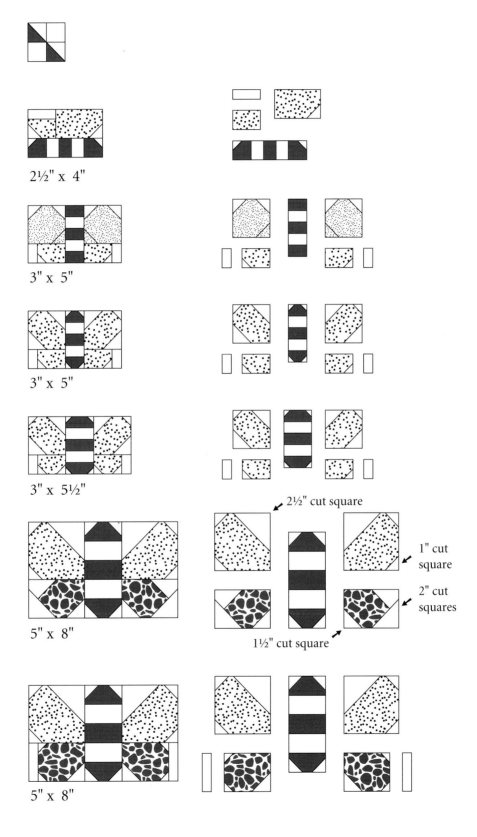

2½" x 4"

3" x 5"

3" x 5"

3" x 5½"

5" x 8"

5" x 8"

2½" cut square

1" cut square

2" cut squares

1½" cut square

Butterflies

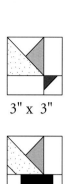

3" x 3"

3" x 3"

Use Marker

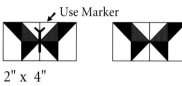

2" x 4"

4" x 4"

 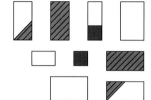

4" x 4"

 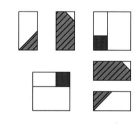

4" x 5"

 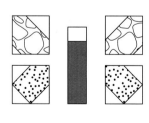

4" x 5"

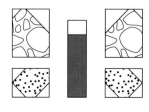

Butterflies (continued)

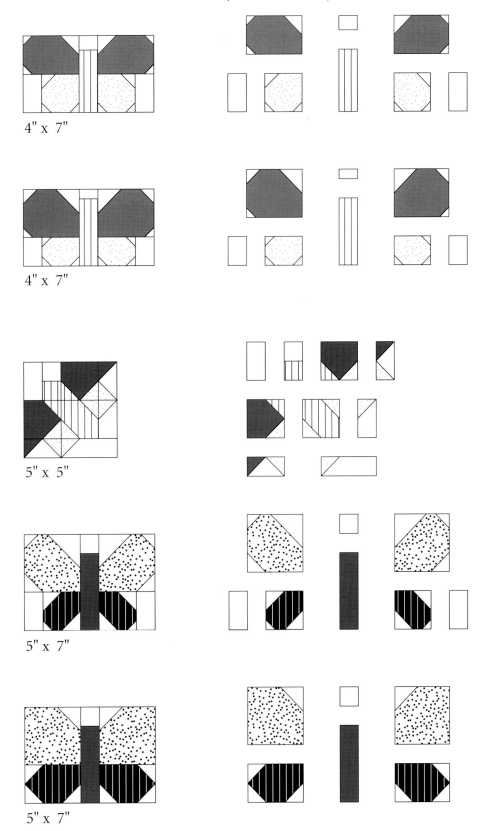

4" x 7"

4" x 7"

5" x 5"

5" x 7"

5" x 7"

Butterflies (continued)

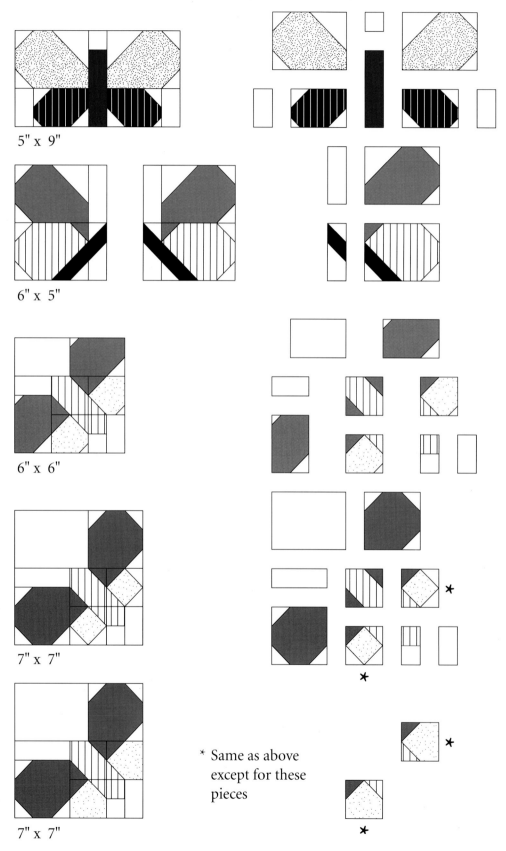

5" x 9"

6" x 5"

6" x 6"

7" x 7"

7" x 7"

* Same as above
  except for these
  pieces

28

Butterflies (continued)

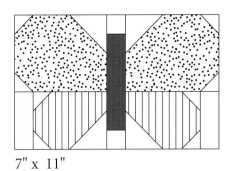

7" x 11"

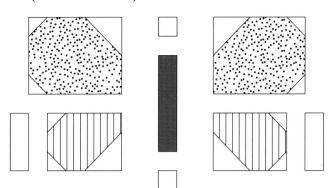

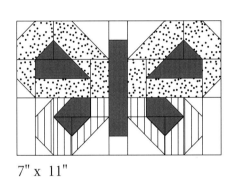

7" x 11"

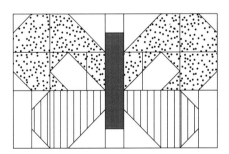

7" x 11"

Design Other Wing Variations

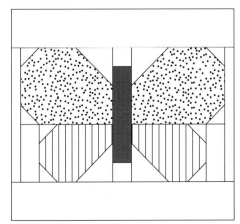

12" x 12"

To Make a 12" x 12" Finished Block

Add cut 1" strips to each side, then
Add cut 3" strips to the top and bottom

Trim block to 12½" x 12½"

Leaves

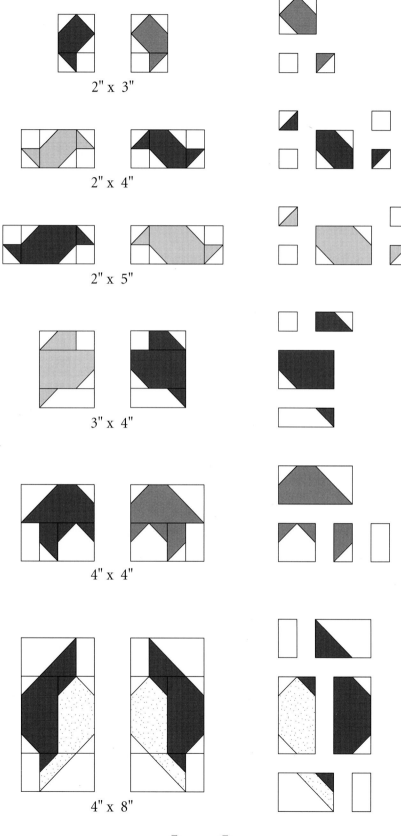

2" x 3"

2" x 4"

2" x 5"

3" x 4"

4" x 4"

4" x 8"

Lilies
Log Cabin Construction

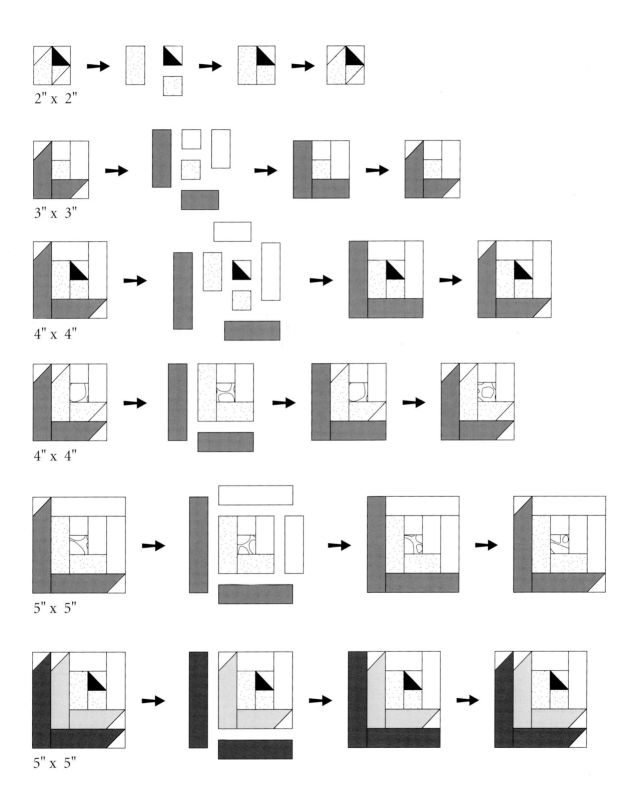

2" x 2"

3" x 3"

4" x 4"

4" x 4"

5" x 5"

5" x 5"

Personal Design Sheet

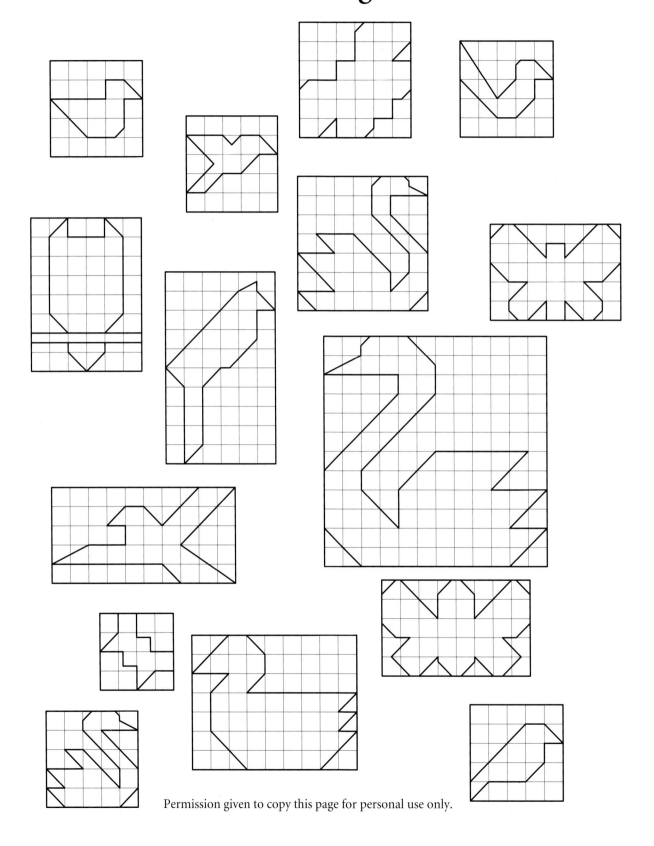

Seagulls at Sunset

37" x 44"

Sea gull blocks were made using background colors that could suggest a sunset.

Seagulls & Waves

39" x 43"

Many variations of this theme are possible using sea gull blocks.

See pattern on page 58.

Nature Silhouettes I

43" x 43"

Black and white images of birds were set against many bright colors.
Using colorful prints for borders makes this a very bright quilt.

This is a variation of the pattern found on page 76.

Butterflies & Lilies
36" x 36"

*Two different butterfly blocks and
log cabin blocks make a colorful
small wall quilt or a large repeat block.
See pattern on page 67.*

A Circle of Doves
36" x 36"

*Many color combinations are possible with
this design (to change the mood).
See pattern on page 56.*

Bluebirds
31" x 41"

*A poster-size quilt that could be made
using many of the other bird blocks.
See pattern on page 69.*

Birds & Leaves
31" x 41"

*The design in this poster-size quilt
could be expanded quite easily.
This is a variation of the pattern found on page 63.*

Swarms of Bees

36" x 36"

Yellow bees create a refreshing contrast to the many white, grey and black prints used for background and borders.

See repeat block on page 78.

A Wreath of Doves

36" x 36"

Dove blocks interspersed with lily blocks could be a Christmas theme if made in different colors.

See pattern on page 57.

Butterfly Magic

60" x 60"

My favorite butterfly quilt. The fabrics and the design details all combine to create a very successful quilt.

See pattern on page 75.

Back of quilt. Two very large butterflies add fun to the back of my favorite quilt!

Large Butterflies

48" x 62"

Any block can be repeated until a quilt of the desired size is created.

38

Nature Silhouette II

29" x 35"

A poster-size version of the theme with white bird silhouettes on cool background colors.

This is a variation of the pattern found on page 77.

Nature Silhouette III

29" x 35"

A poster-size version of the theme with black bird silhouettes on warm background colors.

See pattern on page 77.

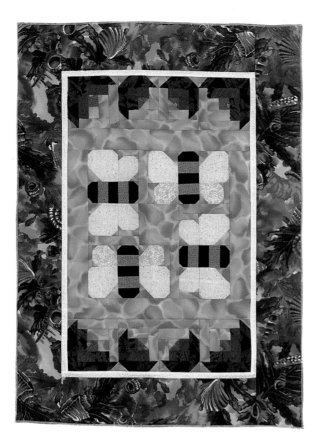

Bees & Lilies

28" x 38"

*Large bee blocks and lilies make
a colorful poster-size quilt.*

See pattern on page 70.

Butterfly Sampler

27" x 41"

*A poster-size quilt made to try out three
different sizes of butterfly blocks.*

See pattern on page 71.

Butterflies

35" x 40"

*Butterflies make a good theme for playing
with color and large fabric prints.*

Wreath of Leaves

43" x 43"

A simple leaf block creates a wonderful autumn theme when made in golds and reds.

See pattern on page 73.

41

Drawn to the Light

37" x 43"

Three different butterfly blocks circle an image representing a light source.

Parrots

32" x 33"

A fun theme because bright colors are always used. Breaking the background down into many fabrics always creates more interest in a design.

See pattern on page 72.

Attic Window

35" x 38"

Color can be added to any of the basic bird blocks so that the birds look realistic. An attic window setting is always delightful.

See pattern on page 65.

Flamingos

32" x 40"

Pink flamingos and white and yellow lilies create a holiday feeling.

See pattern on page 59.

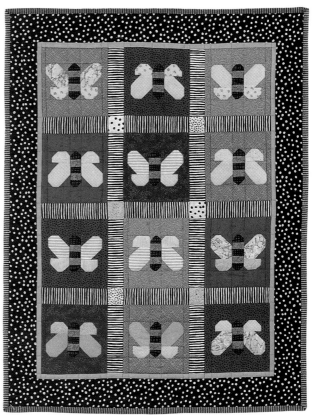

Bees in Flight

26" x 34"

Bee blocks were made using backgrounds of various bright colors. A very pleasing poster-size design.

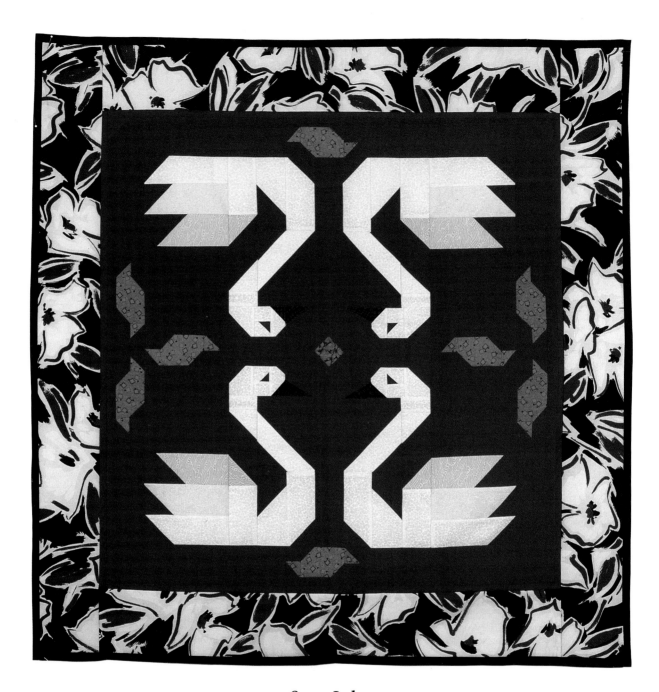

Swan Lake

42" x 42"

*Swans create such a graceful, peaceful image. White swans on a red background
look stunning. A green border could change this into a Christmas quilt.*

See pattern on page 60.

Design and Block
Construction Information

Design Detail Concept

❖ The blocks in this book are made by sewing squares and rectangles together. But before you sew the squares and rectangles together, you will add design details onto the front of the basic pieces.

❖ This could mean adding corner triangles, all the same size, in a repeat pattern. Or it could mean adding corner triangles in selective places during construction of a block. It could also mean adding a variety of design details to one square or rectangle.

❖ When the squares and rectangles are sewn into a block, after many design details are added to the surface, the result is a block that looks very complicated from the front; but from the back you will see only the starting squares and rectangles.

Specific Design Details

❖ *Corner Triangles.* The method used allows you to cut the needed pieces from the strips already cut to make the block. This method also creates accurate squares of half triangles, and is consistent with the way you are adding all design details to the basic squares and rectangles.

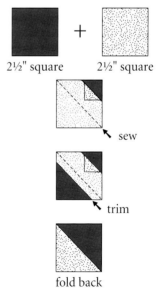

2½" square   2½" square

sew

trim

fold back

Example: To make a 2½" x 2½" half square triangle, cut a 2½" square each of background and design detail fabric. Lay design fabric exactly on top of background fabric, right sides facing. Sew from corner to corner as shown. Press created design triangle to the edge. Trim away middle layer only.

Note: The background square is not cut because the bottom square is an accurate cut, which is important when joining with other pieces. This is consistent with how you make all design details: not cutting background squares or rectangles.

❖ *Corner Triangles Added to Blocks in Progress.* Design details are added to blocks as they are made, not to strips. This is more consistent with working *visually*, adding details as we *see* they are needed.

Example: To add points to log cabin lilies, using 1½" cut strips and log cabin construction, make a 3½" x 3½" (unfinished) lily block as shown. Make points on the two opposite corners of lily fabric. Sew cut 1½" squares of background fabric, right sides facing, as shown. Press created triangles back and trim away middle layer only.

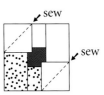

Note: The points should end ¼" from the block edge, so that leaf and flower points are not lost when blocks are joined together.

Note: If the point is lost, use a 1¾" cut square of background fabric instead.

❖ *Use a Variety of Design Details on One Square or Rectangle.*

Example: To make a butterfly wing for the 5" x 7" finished block, use three sizes of background squares to create corners.

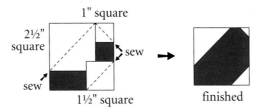

Note: There is flexibility in the block diagrams. Quite often the design details do not have to be duplicated as shown. Experiment with new ideas.

❖ *Simplify Piecing.* Only rarely are squares of half triangles needed. Most often, triangles are created on larger background squares and rectangles.

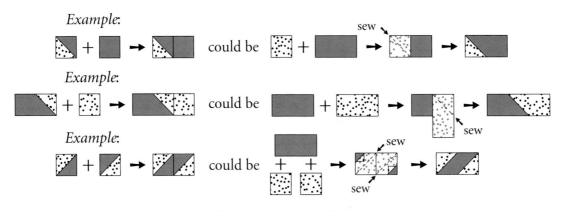

❖ *Advanced Design Detail.* Used in a couple of blocks only.

Specific Instructions for a Block
Reading a pattern:
The 5" x 7" Butterfly

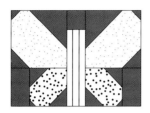

The Finished Block

1. Cut squares and rectangles.

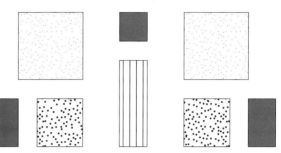

2. Add background design details.

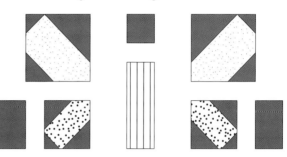

See Construction Example to see the design detail construction concept.

3. Sew squares and rectangles together logically.

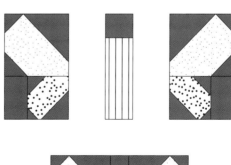

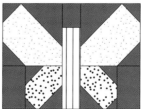

The Unfinished Block (5½" x 7½")

Construction Example
Butterfly Wing

To make the large part of the wing in the 5" by 7" butterfly:

Start with a cut 3½" square of wing fabric.

sew

Cut a 2½" square of background fabric, sew right sides together, fold over and trim middle layer.

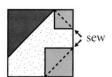

sew

Cut 1" and 1½" squares and attach in the same way.

Unfinished wing part.

Finished wing part.

Using Markers

❖ Using markers on a quilt top was not considered an acceptable practice a few years ago. Times have changed and quilting is a much more liberal and varied field. We are now free to make up our own rules and ways of working.

❖ Changes in the marketplace have also made a difference. There are now many excellent *permanent* for *fabric* markers in different sizes of writing tips widely available. Seeing permanent markers being used to make Baltimore Album blocks loosened up my attitude toward using markers and made me much more willing to add a few design lines with markers.

❖ Adding a few marker lines to a block before sewing it onto a quilt can add quick details that can change and complement the block. Go easy with markers. Do not overdo. This is not a drawn block. It is first and foremost a pieced block, and that should remain the overall impression.

❖ You may also want to consider using hand or machine embroidery instead of markers. With the wonderful sewing machines out now, there are many ways to enhance and add details to these blocks.

Eyes

❖ Eyes are optional in most of the blocks. On small birds and other small blocks, eyes are not worth the trouble of sewing in. On larger blocks (over 6" x 6"), adding an eye is still optional.

❖ Ultimately, all eyes may be drawn in with a marker after the block is sewn together.

❖ For me, an eye is a triangle of fabric created by sewing a square of fabric to a background piece.

Example: Adding a fabric eye to a block. Convert the piece into which the eye is to be placed to small pieces and attach the eye to one of the pieces:

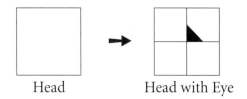

Head   Head with Eye

Beaks

❖ Beaks should be made with strong color in order to stand out. Black, brown, and gold work well.

❖ Most of the bird blocks have a beak shown in the diagram, since most drawings are silhouette images. When sewing the beak design detail, you have some control over changing the size from that shown in the diagram, if you so choose.

❖ If you did not put a beak in a bird block and now decide it needs a beak, use a marker or sewing machine to add this detail. It may be necessary to add marker beaks to very small blocks in order to keep the sewing simple.

Example: To make a long, pointed beak, use a piecing technique similar to that discussed earlier:

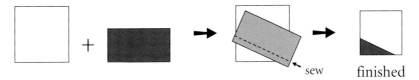

sew   finished

Finishing Techniques

❖ *Square Up.* Squaring up a quilt top means trimming it so that it is square or rectangular and has four 90° angles. This is best done before the final borders are added and/or before the binding is put on.

❖ *Floating an Image.* Most of the blocks in this book look better in a project if the image is floated in background fabric. To do this, add rows of cut background strips, usually 1½", on one, two, three, or four sides of the block.

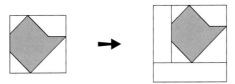

This is also the way to turn a rectangular block into a square block. Square blocks are much easier to design with and to mix with other blocks.

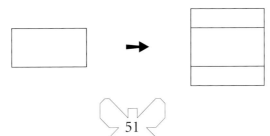

❖ *Creating Larger Blocks.* To make large blocks that may be repeated for a quilt top, start with four small blocks and add strips and squares of background until you have created a square block. In the diagram below is a common method of creating a larger block.

Note: In order to sew in the center square smoothly, five sewing steps will be used, not four.

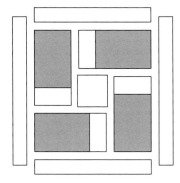

❖ *Machine Quilting.* This was done on all pieces for this book. There are many places on these quilt tops where there are extra layers of fabric. Therefore, machine quilting is advised.

The Patterns

All dimensions in this section
represent *finished* sizes.

Swan Song
26" x 34" (without border)

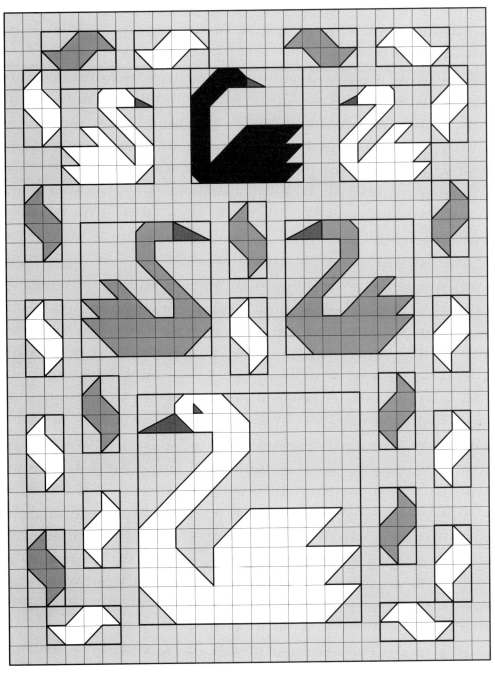

2	5" x 5"	Swans
1	6" x 6"	Swan
2	7" x 7"	Swans
1	12" x 12"	Swan
22	2" x 4"	Leaves

A Circle of Doves
36" x 36"

Christmas - White Doves
- Dark Green Background
- Red Border

Wedding - White Doves
- Purples, Pinks, Yellows

See photograph on page 35.

Wreath of Doves
31" x 31"

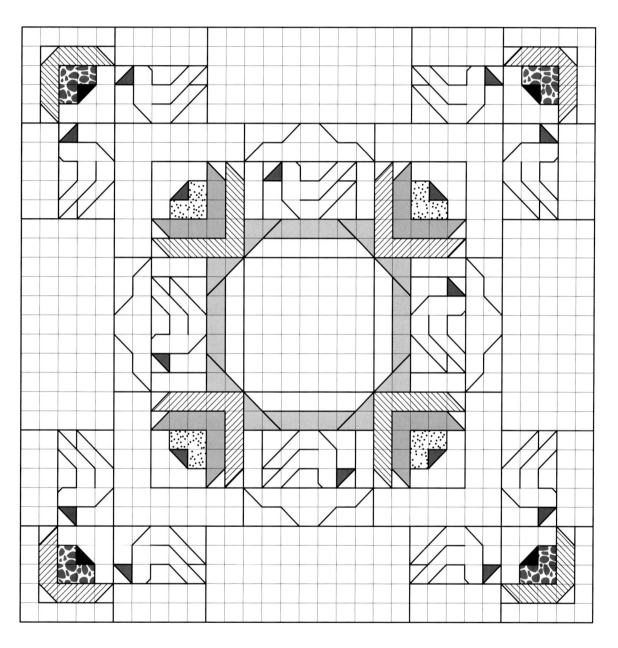

12	3" x 5"	Doves
4	4" x 4"	Lilies
4	5" x 5"	Lilies

See photograph on page 36.

Sea Gulls & Waves
30" x 32" (without border)

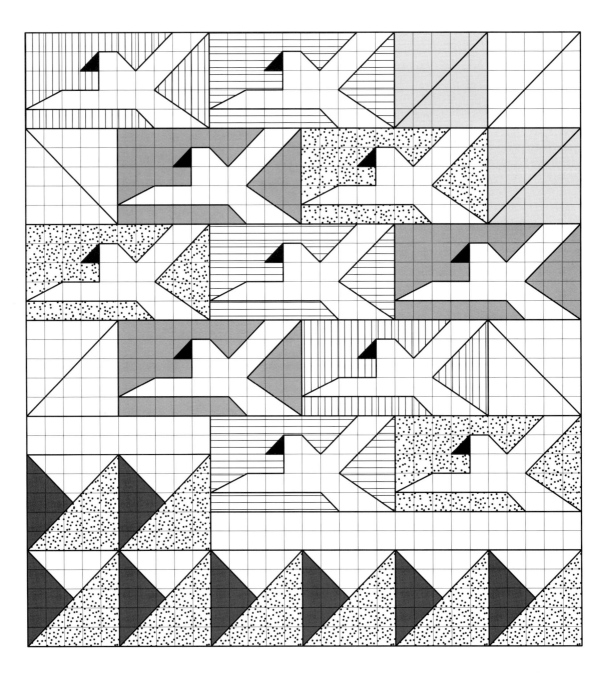

11	5" x 10"	Sea Gulls
6	5" x 5"	Background Sky
8	5" x 5"	Blocks of Waves

Fill in with background

See photograph on page 33.

Flamingos
32" x 39" (including border)

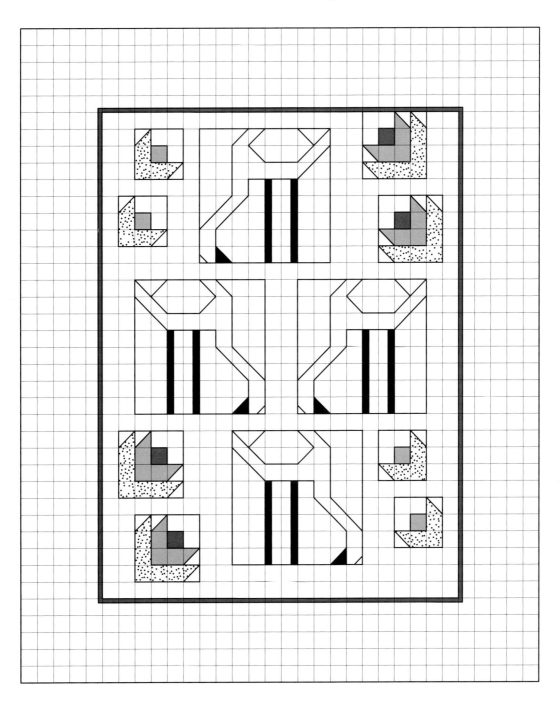

4	8" x 8"	Flamingos
4	3" x 3"	Lilies
4	4" x 4"	Lilies

See photograph on page 43.

Swan Lake

32" x 32" (38" x 44" with border)

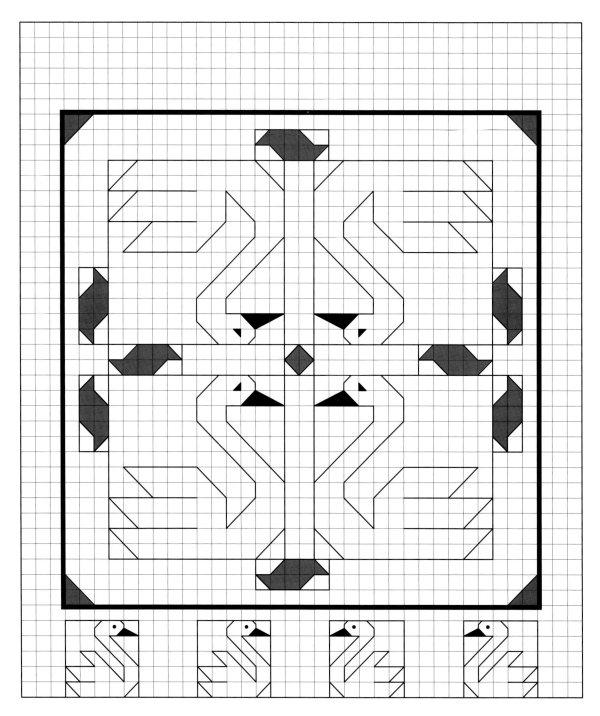

This makes a great baby quilt!
As an option, try 5" x 5" Swans (example above) in the border.

See photograph on page 44.

Ducks Out of Water

23" x 29" (plus border)

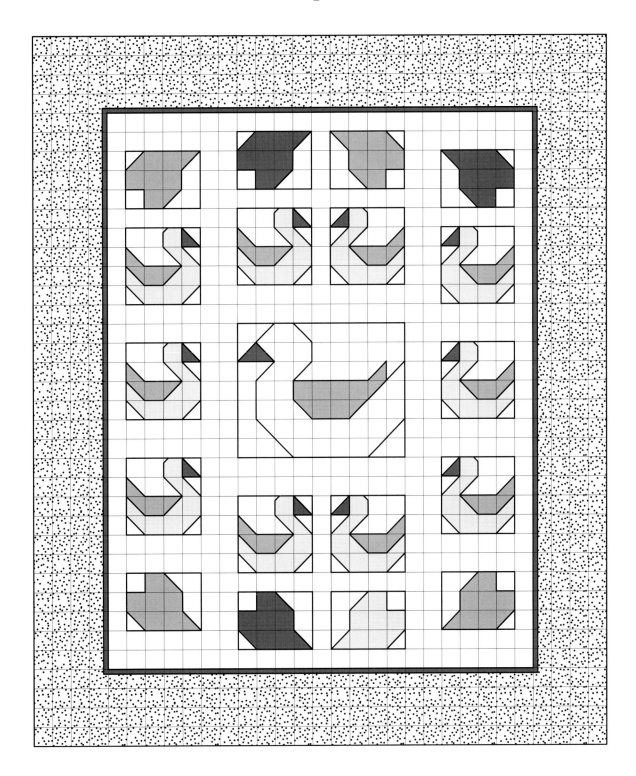

Birds & Flowers*
29" x 33" (35" x 41" with border)

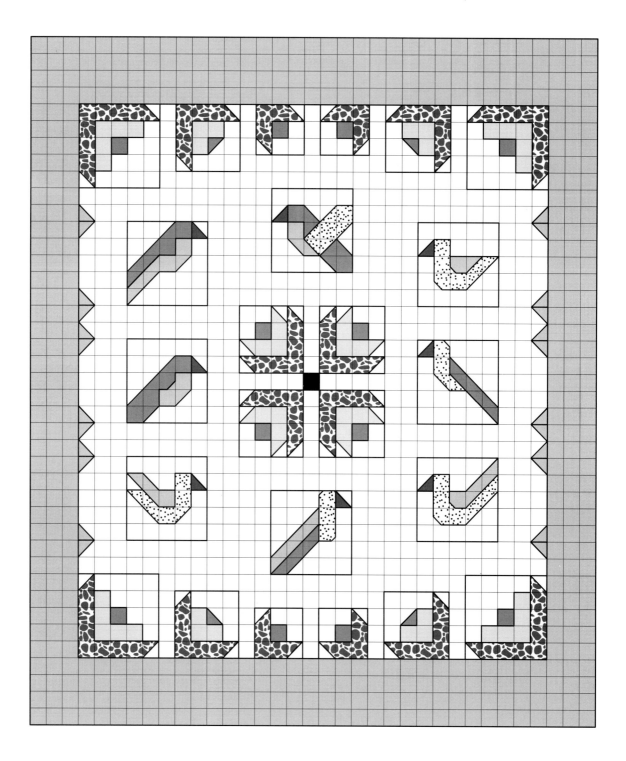

* Option: Butterflies & Flowers

Birds & Leaves
25" x 30" (without border)

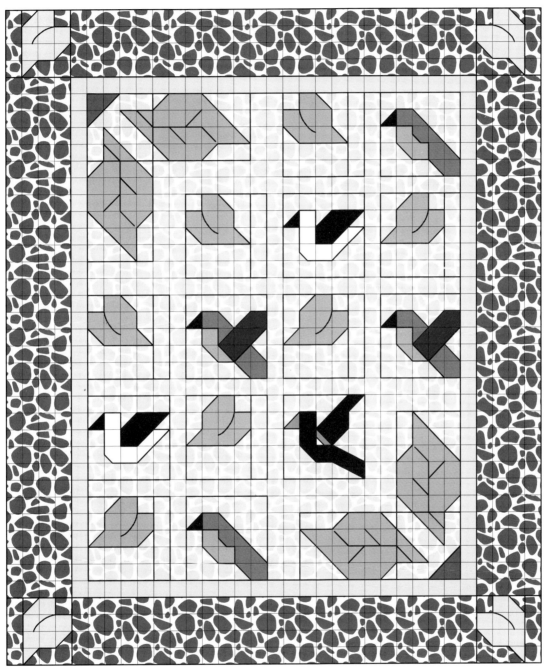

7	5" x 5"	Birds
7	4" x 4"	Leaves
4	4" x 8"	Leaves

For 5" x 5" leaf blocks, add cut 1½" strips to two sides of 4" x 4" leaf blocks.

See photograph of variation on page 35.

Butterflies & Leaves
24" x 28" (including border)
Make a Small Quilt or Use as a Repeat Block

6   4" x 4"   Butterflies
6   4" x 4"   Leaves

Three leaf blocks made in reverse.

Attic Window Sampler
35" x 38"

Use 5" x 5" bird blocks with an extra background strip for the windows.

See photograph on page 42.

Swans
27" x 28" (37" x 38" with border)

8	6" x 6"	Swans
8	5" x 5"	Lilies

Large Butterfly Repeat Block
25" x 25"

4	5" x 7"	Butterflies
4	7" x 7"	Butterflies
4	4" x 4"	Lilies

Option: Add borders for a poster-
size quilt.

See photograph on page 35.

Beehive
40" x 44" (including border)

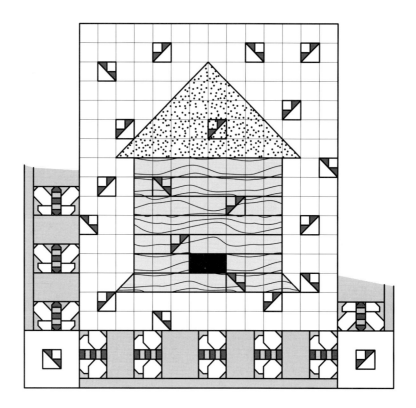

1 square = 2"

Border might include bees as shown here,
   or simple strips.

You might also include bees in the corners.

Bees and More Bees

 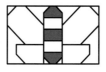 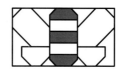 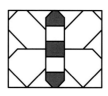

3" x 5"   3" x 5"   3" x 5½"   4" x 5"

Bird Sampler
19" x 31" (without border)

8   5" x 5"   Birds
(2 in reverse)

See photograph on page 35.

Bee Sampler
18" x 28" (without border)

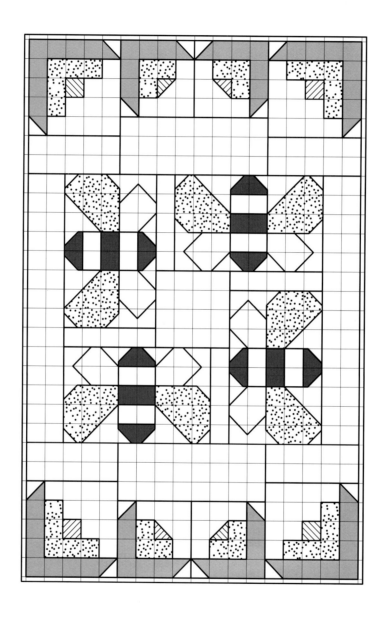

Bees and flowers may be repeated for a larger quilt

See photograph on page 40.

Butterfly Sampler
17" x 31" (without border)

4	5" x 7"	Butterflies
2	5" x 9"	Butterflies

Option: Butterfly Border

See photograph on page 40.

Parrots in Conversation
30" x 31"

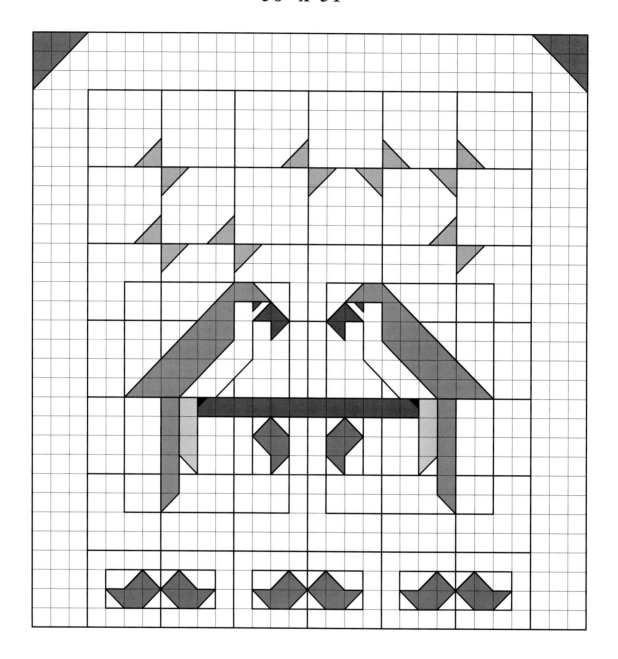

Two Parrots - mirror images of each other

Option: The background is divided into 4" (finished)
squares and a design is added to some squares
to create butterflies and leaves.

See photograph on page 42.

72

Wreath of Leaves

36" x 36" (without border)

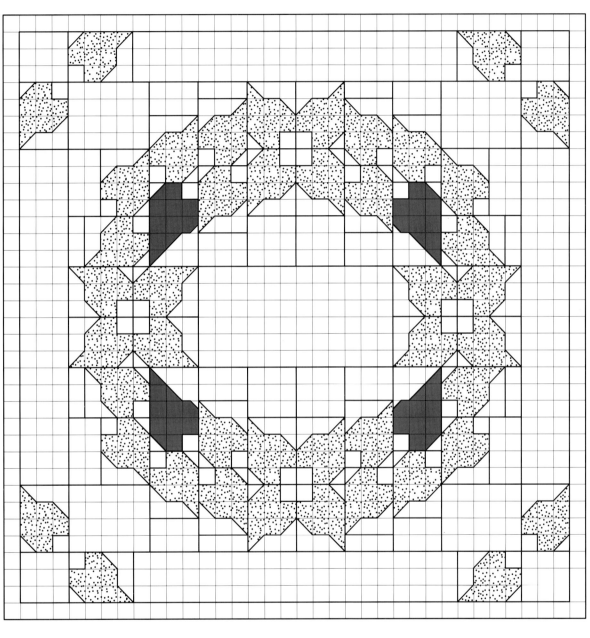

  22 of Each

  2 of Each

See photograph on page 41.

Butterflies & Flowers
A Small Quilt (22" x 22")

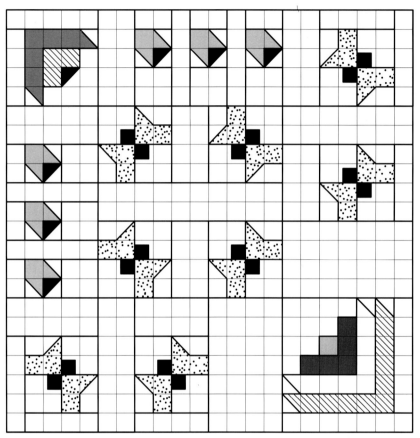

Fill in with cut 1½", 2½", or 4½" strips of background fabric.

...or a Repeat Block

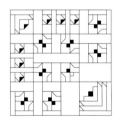
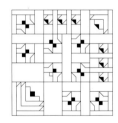

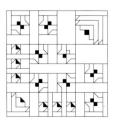
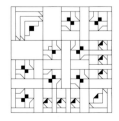

Try four repeats, or, as an option, make two in reverse.

Butterfly Magic

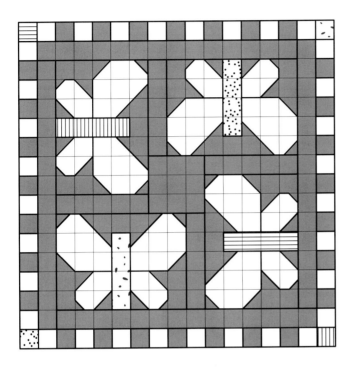

Make a 15" x 15" (finished) block of

4	5½" x 7½"	Butterflies
1	3½" x 3½"	Background Square

1½" cut strips of background for filling in.

Sashing   -   Cut 1½" squares of background fabrics from touching blocks.

12   Different sashing strips made if 9 different backgrounds are used for the 15" x 15" (finished) blocks

4   1½" squares from butterfly body fabrics

4   Narrow borders (cut 1¼" strips)

4   Triangles of border fabric for corners

See photograph on page 37.

Silhouettes of Nature
31" x 31" (without border)

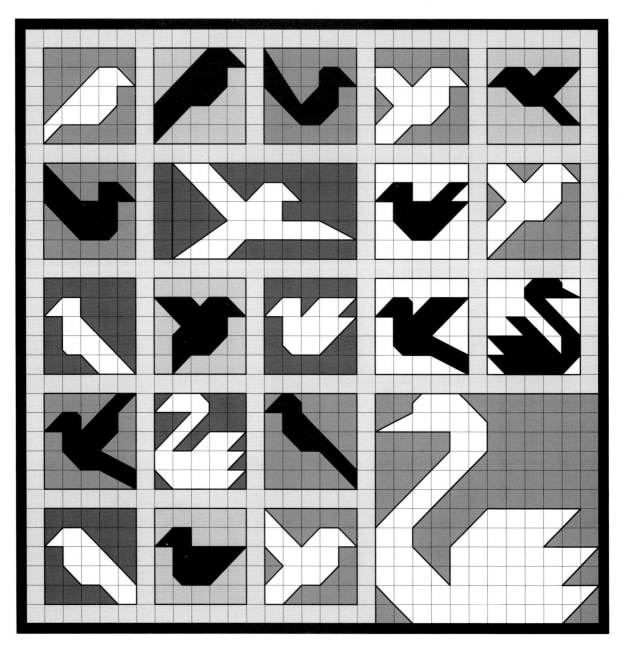

19	5" x 5"	Birds
1	5" x 10"	Sea Gull
1	12" x 12"	Swan

See photograph of variation on page 34.

Small Nature Silhouettes
19" x 25" (plus border)

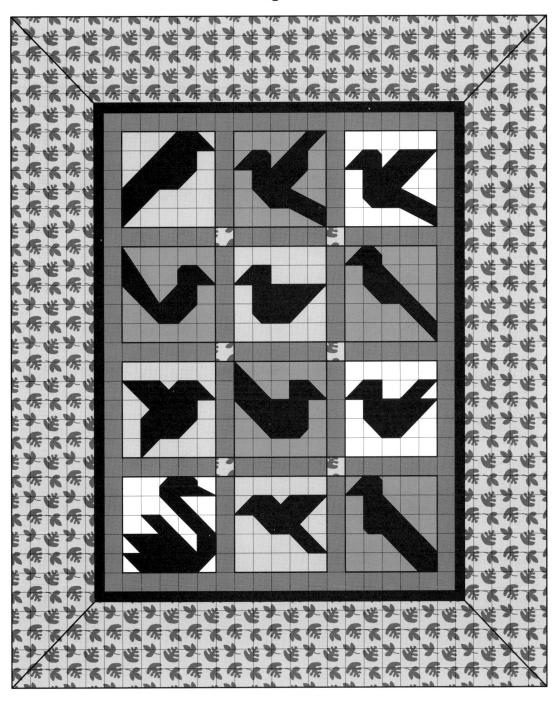

Twelve 5" x 5" Birds in Black or White
Sashing: Cut 1½" Strips

See photograph on page 39.

Repeat Blocks
13" x 13"

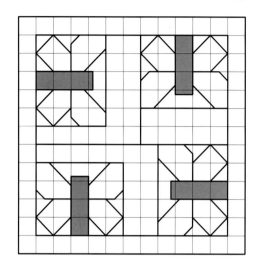

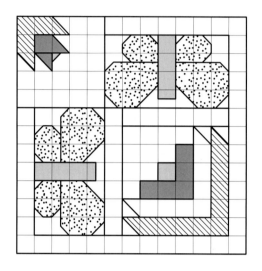

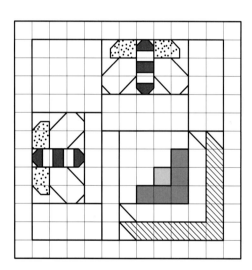

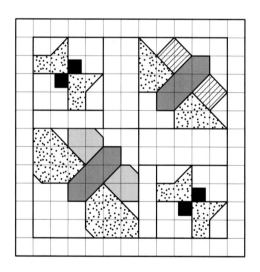

See photograph on page 36.

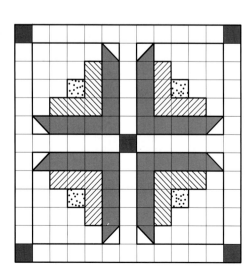

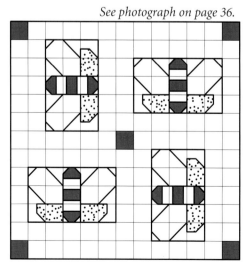

78

Repeat Blocks (continued)
13" x 13"

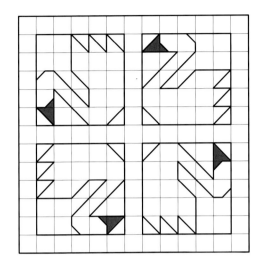
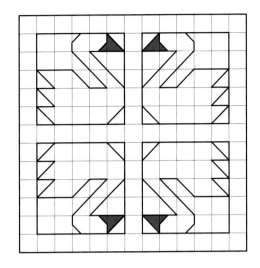

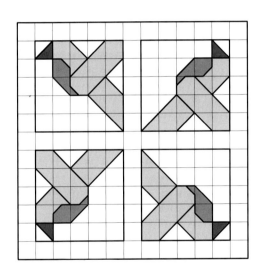
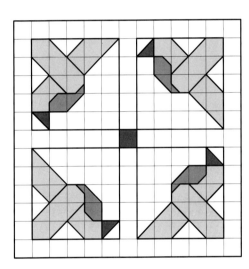

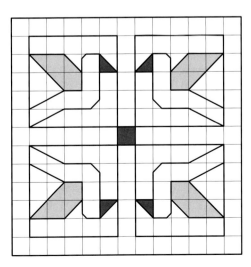
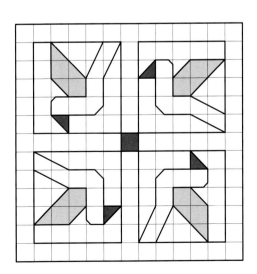

To Bee or Not to Bee
29" x 36" (33" x 40" with borders)

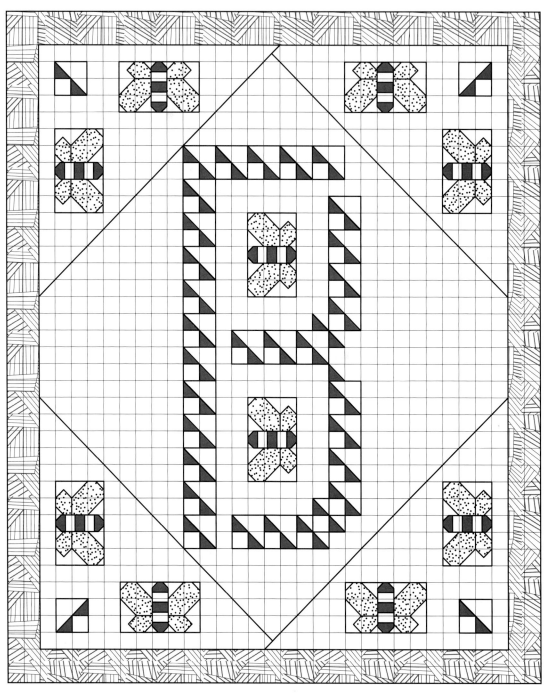

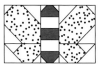

80